STUPID FLOWERS

BY BRICE MAIURRO

Stupid Flowers
© **Brice Maiurro 2017, 2025**

No part of this book may be reproduced by any means known at this time or derived henceforth without written permission of the publisher or author. The exception would be in the case of brief quotations embodied in the critical articles or reviews and pages where permission is specifically granted by the publisher or author.

Books may be purchased in quantity and/or special sales by contacting the publisher. All inquiries related to such matters should be addressed to:

South Broadway Press LLC
1350 Josephine St Unit 102
Denver CO 80206

southbroadwaypress@gmail.com
303.330.8083

Second Paperback Edition, 2025
ISBN: 978-1-7350355-1-2
Library of Congress Control Number: 2025947693

Cover Design: Brice Maiurro
Printed in the United States

CONTENTS_

05 Dresser
06 Several Thoughts on a Fly in My Bedroom Tonight
10 Color Test
12 Mouseketeer
14 Smokes When Drinking
15 I Am Not a Bottle of Pills
17 Reckless
18 Moving Day
21 Today I Drew a Robot
23 Past Lives
24 Whatif
25 There is Something Sad About Today and That is Okay
27 National Anthem of Anywhere
28 The Bardo
30 Dear Maria,
35 Bukowksi #2
36 The Man From The Future
38 Bathroom Stall at King Soopers at Monaco and Leetsdale
39 You Are Not a Flower
43 Phone Calls That I Should Be Making
44 Magic
45 Geronimo
47 Saint Robot
48 Aquarium
49 Tomato
50 It's A Listen to the Beatles on Vinyl in Headphones Kind of Night
52 El Chapo
53 I Blink And
62 The King of His Lawn
64 Organ Music
68 Doing the Dishes
70 Talking to God Over Shitty Coffee at Denny's

72 Conviction
73 I've Drawn You Maybe Fifteen Hundred Times Now
76 Amnistía
78 Woman, Blue Hair
79 Send Me a Postcard
81 We Pretend to Be
84 Quickie
85 Date With a Beautiful Woman (Where I Turn Into a Werewolf)
88 Spies
89 I Slept on Your Floor in the Autumn of Your Home
90 3015 Kalmia
92 I Shot a Bullet at the Mirror and the Mirror Shot Back
93 Sitting in Your Dark Living Room While You Blowdry Your Hair
94 Why Still So Hungry Am I?
96 Heartbreaker
98 Trotsky
99 Bees
101 Xmas
102 An American Portrait
104 Blood on the American Highway
107 Portrait of a Woman at a Gas Station
108 Simon Says
111 Bird #2
112 Bird #1
113 This is Not a Picture Show
116 Waiting Room
117 Ambulance Song
120 Human
122 Seppuku
123 Heaven

STUPID FLOWERS

brice maiurro

poems

SOUTH BROADWAY PRESS
DENVER CO USA

for logan custer,
because you've already
heard all these poems.

Dresser

i've had this dresser for over half my life
wooden, six drawers
little knobs on the drawers
rectangular it is so very rectangular
and i love the thing really i do
it's hard not to love something
that's been so loyal

and in my room
i'm lying on my floor for some dumb reason
and i say to the dresser
"i don't know why i love you, dresser,
you're just a vessel full of all the things
i've gathered,"
and the dresser says
"just like you, asshole."

that was the last time
my dresser and i ever spoke
but i'm not going to get rid of it,
obviously.

Several Thoughts on a Fly in my Bedroom Tonight

1.

as i watch
this fly
land on the beer
on my dresser
he clasps his hands
together

this fly
prays more than
i do

2.

he swarms
around my head
and near my ears
as my blood boils
and i think about
murder

he just wants attention

he just wants
to be seen
and heard
and loved

3.

how come
i never
encounter a fly
when other people
are around?

4.

this fly moves
in a severely unorthodox way
zig-zagging
and writing through the
stale air

either he governs
his own motion
or something else does

he lands
just to take off again
he goes
to the same place
twice

there is a method
to his madness
i don't know what

what keeps him
doing the
same quaint thing
over
and again?

5.

if i swat at him
recklessly
i will never kill him
i have to watch him

i have to understand him
at least a little
if i want to absolve him
of his horrid fly life

(is it horrid?
i can't fly.)

he grows to trust me
it feels like:

he lands on my bed
then the fabric
of my pajamas
then my knee
then my bare chest

6.

after i killed him
i lifted my pillow
where i found him dead

i picked up his lifeless corpse
and his legs moved
             pain—
i euthanized him
from the suffering i began
and set him outside
of my window

i'm not cut out for this

life is so big
and i'm flying desperately
in chaotic patterns
landing in the same spot
over and again

Color Test

displays impatience and
agitation.

feels that life has far more
to offer
and that there are still
important things
to be achieved—
that life must be
experienced
to the fullest.

as a result,
he pursues his objectives
with a fierce intensity
and will not let go of things.

becomes deeply involved
and runs the risk of being unable
to view things
with sufficient objectivity
or
calmly enough; is therefore
in danger
of becoming agitated
and of exhausting his
nervous energy.

cannot leave things alone
and feels he can only
be at peace
when he has finally
reached his goal.

impatient involvement.

over-imaginative
and given to fantasy
and day-dreaming.

longs for interesting
and exciting things to happen
and wants to be admired
for his charm.

the fear
that he may
be prevented from achieving
the things he wants
leads him into
a restless search
for satisfaction
in the pursuit
of illusory
or meaningless activities.

Mouseketeer

and laying in this
thing
place
this
oversized coffin
i think
almost audibly
i am not a poet
i am just a lazy novelist

i am some
american millennial
who wants to be
some
mouseketeer
for the beat generation
because damn
did they stab society in the gut
and because
damn
did they every look cool
smoking those cigarettes

here
in this oversized
coffin

where i love my cobwebs
and the dust that rises
from the floorboards
when i fall as unsober
as life is sobering
against them

i can't quit biting my nails
and i'm far too cheap
for anxiety pills
so i guess i'll just put on
my little black hat
with its little black ears

M-I-C
K-E-Y
M-O-U-S-E

Smokes When Drinking

i wander barefoot into the cold night
little rocks beneath my calloused feet
peacoat and boxers and tipsy
i shuffle through the obnoxious wind
badgering me for bus fare and attention
i disregard the human beings on patios
that stare on from lawn chairs
beneath glowing horsefly light
my shadows morphing, laughing
as i shuffle madly through the evening
i am aware of the monster
that i am right now thank you
headlights and ambulance sirens
death is around i can hear him stalking
but i'm a couple in and i want to smoke
i'm not much of a smoker normally
don't got enough commitment
but i do want my damn cigarettes
and this cost (which is a cost)
is not too high so i push through the void
in search of the vice
to help me to continue to push through
the void

beautiful unsober evening
i am in love with your species
your genus, your family, your order
your class, phylum, kingdom
of love and temperance

I Am Not a Bottle of Pills

i am not a bottle of pills

i am not some sort of
orange plastic container
that you can pull out of your bag
when you are having a bad day
or a breakdown

friendship is not a pair of crutches
that leans on each other

i have hunter in my bones
though there is less blood in my water each day
i do not look to you

i am not built to be a mirror

anymore

so sit beside me
and together tucked in the bushes
we can stare out onto the planes

but you cannot swallow me
i am not drugs

i change too rapidly

i am not claustrophobic
i just like to change rooms
when a door opens

i am not afraid of heights
i just mend my wings before i fly

and when i fall
i crack six ribs as i hit the ground
and i am out
sometimes for months at a time
lost in dreams
and on the backs of nightmares
pushing through jungles
balancing on the hands of a clock
that cannot tell time

and when i arrive
i am glad to see your bright shining face
and i realize you were the sun peeking through the trees
all along

but we are not pills
and if we continue to pressurize ourselves
into tiny capsules
that promise to shake away the haze of life
we will all need disclaimers the length of constitutions

i am not a bottle of pills
but i love you
and if you need someone to listen
never don't ask

Reckless

and as soon as his mother
walked up the stairs
and out of the apartment
he went to the bathroom
grabbed a can of hairspray
he went to the coffee table
grabbed a lighter
and he pointed the hairspray
directly at the lit flame
inches away from the ceiling

i asked him
"logan
what are you doing?"
he pressed the button down
and nothing happened

defeated
he said,
"i just wanted to do something reckless
once in my life,"
and that was the end of that

Moving Day

i have gutted the inside of my heart
thrown out the dusty shit memories
and wrapped the fragile ones
in old newspaper
i separated heartache into a trash pile
and a donation pile
and i threw some guilt into the fireplace
to keep the place warm
since the heat had been turned off

i packed up hope
and when there was room at the top of the box
i tossed in some doubt
to use the box to its full advantage
and i labeled the box
"brice. assorted nonsense."

when we backed the truck in
unlocked and lifted the door
the first thing we packed
was my past
we spent a good half hour
figuring out where to place my conviction
i wrapped the top
of my glass emotions
with some packing tape
so they wouldn't spill on my temper
and catch fire

i nearly broke my back
lifting my self-esteem up the stairs
but a couple friends lent their hands
and of course
i paid them in beer

my awkwardness wasn't heavy
it was just awkward

my dresser drawers were empty
so we filled them with some loose creativity
i didn't really have anywhere else to put it

the drive to the new place was quiet
except for the occasional sound from the back
i was a little worried my soul might have broken
when i heard something scratching
and a loud crash

but we lifted the door to the moving van
and sure enough everything was fine
my ego was a bit bruised
but I don't know if that even happened
during the move

the new place was smaller
i had to put a good friendship in storage for now
but god
someday when i'm wealthier
i mean wealthier wealthier
not wealthier wealthier
i can't wait to take it out

find a place for it
between my laughter and honesty
maybe hang it above a mantel
frame it in trust

we emptied the truck
swept it pretty well
and took it back
and sure enough
empty clean carpet
became the callouses of my feet
white white walls
broke into the ribs of my rib cage
grey dust and brick
lit up like embers of my heart
burning off the boxes we used
to move me somewhere else

Today I Drew a Robot

today i drew a robot

today i went outside in the rain and i laid flat on the ground in the middle of the street
the rain drops fell down and crashed like cymbals on my eyes i did not blink

today i kissed strangers who walked by the other way on the same sidewalk with just my eyes no lips

today i enveloped the entire energy of the moon through a straw with one holy deep sip inward

today i spoke to someone i wouldn't have on a day that was not today it was so everything to know that what i was doing was what i was not before

today i swooned for life and his dreamy blue eyes

today i penciled in an appointment for myself and that looked like fifty cent coffee and vegan tacos and a tallboy and then the aforementioned robot i drew

today i was less cruel
less cruel to other humans and what i found to be true in my truth is with this i was less cruel to myself

today i said no to someone i love because i love them

today i was so far from perfect that i almost circled back it was as if i was walking around the world with giant legs the opposite way of the sun and i caught it

almost

today i drew a robot
and i emphasized the imperfect lines
i emphasized the black circles around his eyes
and in his robot belly i drew a television set
and on the television set was just an image of the robot
and i think that maybe it was a self portrait

and maybe i am an artist but we all are

today i stepped down from the crucifix i nailed myself up to and i realized i don't want to be jesus infamous christ i just want to draw robots and stare up at the rain that stares down at me but just keeps moving

gravity is just vertical motion
into the heart
of the earth
where i long
to be

Past Lives

my friend told me that she wears gold bracelets
because she believes she was cleopatra in her past life

says she has nightmares where she is weeping
for the death of marc antony
or that she is rolled up in a carpet
being smuggled into caesar's palace
she tells me it's where she gets her fire from

i told her that i suspect in my past life i was steve gordman,
an overweight mustachioed used car salesman
from duluth, minnesota in the late 1970s

at times, i wake up in the middle of the night,
and i swear my clothes smell like exhaust fumes
and fried chicken
i believe this is where my mediocre selling abilities
come from

i mean
that's the thing about past lives
if they're a thing, they're not always gonna be winners

sometimes you're cleopatra
and sometimes you're steven gordman
used car salesman from duluth, minnesota

Whatif

i think about what i would do with my time
if i wasn't a writer and i am pretty sure i'd be a carpenter
but i think i'd probably stop halfway through a project
to go lock myself in my room and write poems
because i couldn't focus on carpentry
with all this nonsense floating around my skull
yeah
if i was a carpenter i'd probably just be a poet with a bunch of
wood lying around my house

if i was the president
i'd be a terrible president
but i'd write some brutal poetry

There is Something Sad About Today and That is Okay

there is something sad about today and that is okay
the sun decided to sleep in
the cars they don't move quickly down their thick lines
the news radio is solemn and uninteresting
in the shower i found myself staring at the drain
for way too long
catching up on silly thoughts in my mixtape head
and that is okay
this is all okay

the dynamic of human emotion is dynamic
the hedonists may be will be filled with disappointment
on this one
but not every day is a party
maybe today was the day i was designed
to count the sidewalk blocks
as i walked by hundreds of displaced human beings attempting
to sleep in the entry ways of local business shops

it is a mistake to think your existence is one of exuberant joy
your existence is rocket ship, yes, probably
but so many tiny broken hands pieced together your engine
so many people stood around just to watch you launch

it only makes sense if you acknowledge
the collective experience of us all
maybe god is the devil and humanity has to be its own god

we still haven't figure out how to combat natural disasters
we still haven't figured out the most efficient and effective
methods of loving one another

so if there is something sad about today then that is okay
this dream is far too valuable to be perfectly utopian
let's just try to keep our rocket ships directed toward
whatever it is above us now
that we find so valuable

National Anthem of Anywhere

beautiful land!
you are the only
beautiful land for me
this is where i live

our bright history
our human roots
our sense of pride
for our sense of pride
it is for you i make
some sacrifice

when things get
somehow difficult
you continue on

we believe in these values here

you are where i live
so for you, i love you more
i will die
for the perspective of life
that you
have thrust upon me!

the only one
i've ever known

The Bardo

it's strange to think that there is someone above my head right now. that as i lay here in bed that someone is just floating above me, playing guitar terribly, maybe in a chair. it's strange to think we've crossed paths in halls and that's not significant, or at least we've decided it's not.

i just passed by a woman at the coffee shop watching porn. just neatly watching two naked women go at it, her hands neatly in her lap. and i think maybe she's allowed to do that. i'm not harmed. i'm almost indifferent, yet on the flip side it's worth noting as i've never seen a woman at a coffee shop watching porn before.

the thing about old jazz music is you know that the people performing it are dead. it's strange to think that their breaths were recorded. that i'm hearing their dead people breaths through brass. it's strange to think i love it.

i don't really think i know how to write a poem. a lot of days i sit down and i feel like how i imagine those people who tried to put together an ikea set on acid felt like. poems aren't really tangible. old poems always sound angsty.

it's strange to think that i watched a movie of an actor playing basquiat painting a painting and then after that, i watched a documentary with footage of basquiat painting that painting. and now, years later, it's strange to think i've seen that painting. they don't want you to touch the paintings because they need to preserve them, but i think it's probably for the best because i don't know that i could handle it.

it's too available. all of it. it's all too available. i quit my job after six years and right now i could do pretty much anything and a large portion of my time goes to putting game pieces on the monopoly board for the contest my grocery store is running. it's strange to think we can do just about anything. and we don't just have the now. we have the then. the basquiat painting, the brass breath of dead jazz musicians, the incredible freedom to call a poem whatever we want to. there's indifference to a woman in public watching two previously recorded women have sex. we're all one and we're all connected but that's not just beautiful. in a sense it's kind of unbearable. like putting together an ikea set on acid. i am seven billion humans, a bunch of trees, a lampshade, a beatles song in reverse, an episode of "everybody loves raymond".

i am brass breath from a dead trumpet.

there might be someone over my head
it might be god, it might be you

Dear Maria,

dear maria,
i do not know who you are
but somehow you've snuck your way into my poetry
so here we go

maria,
as you go out into the night
make sure to wear your coat
hold up
i'm not your fucking father, maria
do what you want to

maria,
this may not be easy
you and me
we hardly know each other
but i have to write you a poem

dear maria,
there's a lot of people in this world
probably too many
the thing about people is
they really like to have sex
and sex without protection feels better
but it also creates more people
god is all about the conundrums

dear maria,
are you god?
you might be
i don't know you

but i'm certain you are out there
and i feel compelled to talk to you

dear maria,
remember that in the scheme of things
we are the youngest people to ever live
and more people have died for you
than any time in history
assuming you prescribe to the concept of
linear time
but i feel like that's important
either way
be grateful
when you're hungry
be grateful
when you feel you've got it all
and you did it all yourself
be grateful
people drop dead all the time
also don't fear death
or the idea that you could drop dead
right now

why am i compelled to give you advice, maria?
maybe i should shut my mouth and listen to you
put my ear to your seashell heart
and hear the ocean

assuming you have a heart
maybe you're a jellyfish
i think jellyfish don't have hearts
do you know, maria?

maria,

promise me this
sit on a wooden floor
with headphones on
and listen to a record player
don't let it move the needle for you
move the needle for yourself
if there is no heaven
this is heaven
we are pretty good
at synthesizing our dreams
in the face of the fear
that they may not come true

dear maria,
your heart will be broken
by an asshole
and you will be an asshole
and break someone's heart
and then there's another heartbreak too
oh yes there's several kinds
but the kind i'm thinking about is the one
where neither of you was an asshole
when there's just white noise between you
and you have to step away
that one has its own flavor of hurt
be ready for that one
but you can't be
just a warning
a borderline useless warning

and plus
you might be old and wise and full of heartbreak
maria
tell me about your heartbreaks
are you in a place to tell me about your heartbreaks?

dear maria,
get dessert at salad buffets
another good option
is to avoid salad buffets

dear maria,
i want to dance with you
not romantically
well maybe
but i think i want to dance with most people
people should dance more
and sing more
it drives me nuts that people give me strange looks
when i sing while i'm walking
keep singing
do not reduce yourself to humming
or whistling
avoid silencing your songs at all costs

but also
enjoy awkward silences
(

)
i have mastered them
i plant my garden in their empty plot

no maria,
i am not on drugs
i am just a poet
and it's one in the morning

dear maria,
do not underestimate strangers

acquaintancy is the canvas of
strange sincerity
sometimes you can only unload
your hot irrational jukebox tracks
on bus stop furniture people

i love you, maria
that might not be real love
but right now it's pretty good

dear maria,
i cannot decide if i am sincere and dramatic
or facetious and random

have fun out there
writing with crayons on the walls of time
and throwing things into the void

hold onto this poem

Bukowski #2

i wonder
if bukowski
wrote
so
many
of his poems
like
this
because
he knew
that
publishers
paid
by
the
line.

The Man From the Future

i was on the light rail one day
didn't know where i was headed
just one of those days where the sun
wasn't gonna come into the house
so rather than waiting for the
floodwaters of introversion to rise
i rode my bike over to the train
and hopped on towards denver
away from the television and the bed
and there across from me on the train
was a young boy, maybe 9 years old
in a business suit, reading the paper
he read from it with the focus of a monk
turning the pages in established ritual

excuse me i said to him
he looked at his watch then up at me
"it's 9:47,"
no no no i said
i was just going to ask
aren't you a little too young to be
on the light rail alone
"too young?" he inquired
with a stern gaze
yes, i said
you must be no older than 10
you're just a boy
"i am not a boy," he said,
"i am a man from the future."

he'd stolen my tongue
i wanted to say—
and i'd wanted to say—
but i ended up not saying
because he was telling the truth
and in that moment
the glare of the sun
piercing the train windows
i felt as if
i was just a boy from the past

Bathroom Stall at the King Soopers on Monaco and Leetsdale

on one wall of the bathroom stall
at monaco and leetsdale
someone took the time
to carve an upside down crucifix into the wall
beneath which they carved
"FUCK GOD. GOD IS EVIL."

to which another stranger retorted
"IF GOD IS EVIL
THEN THE ONLY TRUTH
IS DEATH"

someone in agreeance
circled the world "DEATH"
and added "EXACTLY!"

another someone put
"THESE PEOPLE NEED GOD IN THEIR LIVES"

and one person
holiest of them all
wrote
"I'M JUST HERE 2 POOP"

Hallelujah. Amen.

You Are Not a Flower

you are not a flower.

you do not rise
from the soil
like some dandy little
spark of life

you are not
overflowing
with green vanity

you just are.

when spring hits

you do not bloom

you do not rise up

from the cold winter

to burst forth into
some spectral showcase
of expressionistical color

you are not some
kaleidoscopic
manifesto

you are not
in constant competition
with the bright roses
around you

you are not
in constant praise
of the sun

your tongue is not
held out before you
drinking in
the ultraviolet rays
you've been fed

you do not
think of your roots
as being for
gathering life
into your body
like stranger prayer

you are not a flower.

you bloom inward
you burn circles
in your living room rug

trying to find
unidentified life lying
in the widening crack
of your ceiling

you lick the salt
from your wounds
and watch your hands
swell

you waste days
you boil water into boredom

you've torn your roots
from the bureaucratic soil
of bureaucracy

lifted
your two-dimensional legs
from the blueprint
they laid out for you

and you're not always
so beautiful

you don't have
the distinct privilege
of a best laid plan

you are something else

seedless
fruitless
without petals

you dance best drunk
and to heavy metal

you are not a flower.

you are the crayon
that walked to the edge
of town
and outside of the lines

and when you bloom
it'll be in the middle of winter
in the middle of the night
and you will not bloom delicate

you, my dear
will bloom fists and fury

Phone Calls That I Should Be Making

days like today i can just
see it

the sky cracks open
ominous and glowing
and we realize

that we all have just
been living
on the inside of an
enormous blue egg

the whites of the
blue oceans run loose
into a frying pan mixed
with the inner core yolk
and we are cooked
with butter
and spinach
ooh and mushrooms
maybe some feta cheese

wow

we might be an omelet
soon

i have some phone calls
to make

Magic

they paid no mind
to the prophet in the street
as they purchased their tickets
to see a man in a suit
pull rabbits out of a hat

Geronimo

he lived in his car over the winter
he was a point on the grid but far from the line of best fit
he never let anyone else pay
he looked like he hadn't eaten for days
but he always had an unhealthy bundle of generosity
in his wallet
he stepped on every single sidewalk crack
he bummed cigarettes from everybody constantly
and no matter how stressed he got
no matter how much the veins in his skull bulged
he always refused to smoke an american spirit

he was a smoker
like some people are hipsters
or gutterpunks or catholics
he was a smoker
that was his defining factor
the way he would drain a 100
as if that was the whole point of the exercise
he kicked dirt wherever there was dirt to be kicked
he questioned the stars
he yelled fuck you! to the stars
fuck you moon!
fuck you space!
he was at war with humanity
he never won

he slept on the light rail
he slept behind mutiny now
of course he smoked while he slept
but it was one giant motion for him

there was no ritual
you just went until you couldn't anymore
and then you crashed til you woke
sometimes he'd just fall off the face of the earth
it made you worry about him the first couple times

when he spoke from the heart
he was like a shithead fairy godmother

he never existed
if he did i didn't know him
but he has a lot of shitty qualities
that i wish that i had
the end.

Saint Robot

if i were a giant robot
i wouldn't ravage the city;
that is just a stereotype
of giant robots.

i would just sit and meditate
in the middle of
central park.

i'm sure a few park-goers
would be crushed
beneath the extreme weight
of my shiny metal ass.

look
i'm a giant robot
trying to obtain enlightenment,
i'm not a saint.

Aquarium

i went to the aquarium recently
and as i stood there staring at the jellyfish,
the eels, the sharks all pushing through the water
on the other side of the cinematic glass
i saw a boy
and he stared right back at me

he did not swim
he did not wear any kind of apparatus to help him breathe
he just walked across the floor of this
small segment of the ocean like a polaroid photo where he
ended where the edges were, he moved in blurs
like someone shook the photo too hard
amongst the aquamarine blue depth he just stared back
we did not speak but we heard everything we said to each other
we remained in constant conversation for a short eternity

as i walked away he walked away too
out of this snapshot of the ocean
and back into the sunlight where my gills disappear
and i am just and only and less than
but the boy in the aquarium and i
we both know better than that

Tomato

there is a hole in the heart
sure
but it's less of a gravel pit
and more of a dark star
internally endless
worlds and cities
fall in
the eyes of lovers
fall in
the benzadrine-driven
scrolls of philosophy
fall in
suns are born and die
within it
and in its space
is patient nothingness
waiting to be filled
with chaotic structure
or structured chaos

well
okay
yeah yeah
same difference
tomato tomahto

It's a Listen to the Beatles on Vinyl in Headphones Kind of Night

after a
walking home in the cold without a jacket
kind of day

where i talked to
god, you love to hear yourself talk
kinds of people

who have
i am passionate about reality t.v.
kind of personalities

when all i want is a
this is just life; hold on and don't fall asleep
during the pretty parts
kind of vibe in the air

or a
sitting alone drinking whiskey and reading whatever it is
in my hands
kind of afternoon

where
i have way better shoes than all of you
kinds of people are missing

when the air is
i don't know what temperature or density this air is,
but i fucking love it
kind of air

it's a
whatever we feel like
don't stop for hitchhikers
command your troops to battle
pretend to love your enemies
kiss and tell
morning-after pill
age-defying cream
music video marathon
green grass
with a body in the basement
eight-bit delusion
fix yourself
kind of world.

when all i want is a
listen to the Beatles on vinyl in my headphones
kind of night

El Chapo

but part of me wants to root for
a drug lord named el chapo
who dug his way out of prison
and is on the lam
somewhere in mexico

there's a certain romance
that blooms its petals
over the thorns of giving a shit

I Blink And

i blink and
one million people pass by me
at one million miles per hour
as stupid flowers bloom
and brilliant cities are planned
and corrupted
and born again
from the genesis of tragedy

i love in the moment
i mean
i try
but i get lost at sea
with my technology
and my telescope
that can see the wall
at the end of the universe but
only from the perspective
of my sight

and there
sitting on the wall
at the end of the universe
is a manic pixie dream girl
my answer to questions
i should be able to answer on my own
but unfortunately
not all of us are born
philosophers and tech gurus
some of us are just born
starry-eyed idiot boys
forced to pace around our rooms
for 40 days

with no water no oxygen
not an ounce of television
just us our love
and the exhaustion of staring at the
ceiling

i wander drunkenly down the halls of
harvard
i love voraciously as i fall asleep in a bathtub
in your heart
i drive myself insane trying to recreate
the something that maybe
but possibly
maybe not?
i fall asleep with a lampshade
on top of my enlightened head
in the bathtub
of your heart

i blink and
i am lost in some sea of angelic
monsters

i blink and
i am shooting downtown
in a metal death shuttle
piercing the skin of denver

i blink and
i am lying in bed
reading 10,000 pages
of a murakami novel
not about you
my room was hit

by a tornado
and i really couldn't
give a shit

i blink
and my sister is marrying
the man of her life
i blink
and she is rosy-cheeked
and happy
and barefoot
and pregnant
and still in love
and she cries at her son's
graduation
and she holds her husband's
hand
and i blink and i
blink
and i blink
and

i channel surf
the million lives i want to
live
and don't think about
pink elephants
you're thinking about pink elephants
aren't you?
and don't think about death
oh wait

i blink and
i am driving to saint joseph
to save my lover

i blink and
i am playing pinball
until four in the
imaginary morning

i blink and
i am in the car crash arms
of my saint joseph lover

i blink and
i am playing the white album
backwards

i blink and
i am swimming in my mother's
chicken noodle soup

i am swimming
in a bathtub
in a hotel room
in your heart

i am charismatic
and charming
and almost out
of anxiety pills

i am down to
my last
anxiety pill

i am
my anxiety pills

i just
don't know
who what where

when
why i am
at the moment
in the
sand dunes
in a hotel room
in your heart

i blink and
i am billy pilgrim
who has come
un
stuck in
time

against my
mother's wishes
i have stared too long
into the eternal sunshine
of the spotless
mind

i am
jim carrey
in eternal sunshine of the
spotless mind

i am
kate winslet
in eternal sunshine of the
spotless mind

i am
hiding from
the velociraptors of reality
in an oven
on a dinosaur island

i am love
(i should always take a
moment to remember that
because it reminds me
that there is no such thing as
incorrect or irrelevant
or unimportant
you are important
you are too important
and the things that
you say
create waves that last
long after the moon
has blacked out drunk
remember that)

remember how beautiful
you looked
in my rearview window
as i went so very
not fucking gentle
into that good night

i blink and
i am watching my friends
sail away from the shores
of colorado
into the distorted audio
of california
into the arms
of jack daniels
into the eyes
of spiritual materialism
into the death star

i blink and
i am wallflowering
so very well
i am so very good
at wallflowering
when i want to
wallflower
and for the longest
i felt terrible
about wanting to
wallflower
but if time
the liar
has taught me
anything
it's that i'm allowed
to wallflower
we move
so fast
even when
we're not in
motion

i blink and
i am beneath your version
of the stars

i blink and
i am doctor gonzo
on a two-week
sociology binge
where the windows
are shattered
and the doors have
been busted open
and i am taking notes
on the human disease
and its beautiful
afflictions

i blink and
i am listening to a
tape recording of your voice
telling me nice things
about myself
and i am still
out of anxiety
pills

(i blink and
i turn off the lights
and listen to
something
and i meditate on
how people would speak
if words were as expensive
as college)

i blink and
call my mom and dad
on my way home from work
in zero degree temperatures
in november where i live
to tell them i love them
and i want to see them
(and i want to see you)
soon
i'm sorry i've been busy
and feeling very anxious
and honestly
i feel like if i blink anymore
i might miss

The King of His Lawn

see him
just across the way there
leaning on his cane
and smoking his cigarette
in his white plastic throne; he
is the king of his lawn
and his kingdom runs
as far as his
fading eyes
can see.

he waters his garden
he trims the weeds, he
pillages his dynasty with
the blades of a lawnmower that roar like
the armies of his backbone.

he
is the king
of his lawn.

high ruler of
this kingdom
and he surveys
and he makes the decisions
and he brings his
portable radio out with him
and listens to what
the rest of the world is so obsessed with
listens to

what the world is doing
as he stubbornly becomes
a gargoyle
serving and protecting his people
of which
he hasn't any.

but you can tell
by his beaten-up
wife-beater
and his pristine blades of wet grass
and the dying look in his eye
as he watches you walk by
that he
is the king
of his lawn.

Organ Music

it's not always gonna be
some bullshit disney symphony

most the time it's not

it's organ music
glass smashed in yer palm
some hidden maestro
in the depths of yer liver
playing doom and gloom

and honestly
that's the good stuff
that's the stuff you want

because here's the thing
it's a shame to close your eyes
for the drop

put yer goddamn hands
in the air

that feel good old timey music
is a bunch of dead people
they were once oxygen thieves too

once pearly whites
and ivory gloves on the teeth
of the piano

carefully avoiding
the black keys

once all sweet love song
and they probably felt it too
it's a good one

have you felt it?

have you come up on love
hands shaking
eyes all tremors and broken breath?

and then bam
yer there
liquid ecstasy

unadulterated honesty

but oh the comedown
the second fall

the rekindling
of time
with structure
without
sweet distraction

no flowers
at yer doorstep
just eviction notice
last call to make pay
or evacuate the reality
you forget about

welcome back
this is the face of
heartbreak

this is where you build muscle

this is the part
where you turn down the lights
step into the doldrums

and play organ music

and how fucking gorgeous it is
how raw how honest
grain cereal—no prize at the bottom

just echo

those rusty golden pipes
churning scar to scab
churning misery to wisdom
ugly little honesty
churning the fade to black
into this grand giant loud
obnoxious crescendo
that screams

through the illusion
that you exist
and this
this here organ music
it matters

Doing the Dishes

on a sunday afternoon
white light peaks into the window
as i scrub cheese off of a plate
peanut butter out of a bowl
rinse tea from a coffee cup
when the water gets backed up
i run the garbage disposal
and watch as it all fades away
into whatever is on the other side
the kitchen is dim and quiet
my feet bare and sticky on the floor
i am at peace
and then bam

a flash overcomes me
and my third eye opens
suns and moons spiraling within it
i see the everything
and the everything sees me
my arms become giant wings
my heart grows into a great garden of trees
my feet lift from the sticky ground
my eyes roll back and my pruned finger tips
touch the clouds touch the ribcage of god
i am one with the nothing
and the nothing is one with me
my bloods rages with true compassion
my breaths grow deep

i breathe in the green grass of kyoto
i breathe out the smokestacks of america
i am a great beacon of all that ever was
and all that ever will be
and then i realize we are out of dishwasher detergent
and i should run by the store to get some.

Talking to God Over Shitty Coffee at Denny's

like two in the morning or something
i couldn't sleep so i called up God
and was all like "hey God,
do you want to meet up for some coffee?"
and God of course obliged me like always
so we're sitting around Denny's
drinking shitty coffee talking when i ask God
"is destiny a thing?" and God says "yes,"
and i say "that's kind of a bummer,"
and God says "well, i don't think that doesn't mean
you can't be proud of the decisions you make,"
and i say "i guess,"

and then there's an awkward pause,
the waitress comes by
refills our coffees
and we sip in silence and then i say
"alright, God, what number am i thinking of?"
God says 3.
it was 3.
What am I thinking now?
God says i'm thinking about destiny
and i was like
well yeah okay that might not have been the
best approach and then i took the salt shaker unscrewed the lid
and poured the entire thing of salt into my cup of coffee.
God says "why did you do that?"
and i say "you seem surprised.
i thought you knew that i was going to do that?
wasn't it part of my destiny?"
and God was like
"no - that shit just came out of nowhere."
i think God would have turned to God for answers in that
moment if that made any sense.

and then i held God's hand
and i said
look. i know what they say.
man plans and God laughs and that's beautiful
but sometimes we just take the car off cruise
control and we start driving off the road in the middle of
Nebraska and we're pushing through the corn fields and doing
donuts and blasting dizzy gillespie and it makes no damn sense
and no one could have seen it coming, not even you, i'm sorry,
but that's why i put the salt in the coffee because some things
weren't written.
some things happen that weren't meant to happen and those
things were meant to happen but not in the sense that everyone
saw it coming because
sometimes no one sees it coming.
even you, God.
sometimes it's brutal and vicious hard work or a spark to the
heart and it's raw and honest and it's tangential and that tangent
shoots off into space like a monkey in an astronaut suit and it
forms a new monkey planet with a new monkey God who too
will have a moment of awe when realizing that your
children are not you.
they break the rules in the name of something.
love
or change
or dizzy gillespie
but yes.
it's a thing that happens and it'll catch us all off guard.

and then the waitress stole the cash in the register, took off her
apron and busted out the door into the cold night.

Conviction

conviction
is important
but if ever
you decide
to wrestle a bear
or halt a moving train
or cheat on love
you may find
these things
have more
conviction
than you.

I've Drawn You Maybe Fifteen Hundred Times Now

i've drawn you maybe fifteen hundred times now

i've drawn you naked
resting in the sandpaper palm
of my open hand

i've drawn you staring into forever
licking blood from your lips

i've sat and i've sketched
every singular ounce of your curves
onto the sistine chapel ceiling
of my unholy skull

every fogged breath against
the window pane of my cornea
every scratch against my retinal walls

i've drawn you like a pair of scissors
drawn out then back together
sharp blades dancing against the friction
of one another

i've drawn you like the paper that they cut

i've drawn you like snow
falling onto cardboard boxes in some back alley
that doesn't exist

i've drawn you like time
abstract and mechanically lost
graphite swirls extending across paper edges
onto tables like dust

i've drawn the forest
that runs through the spaces between my bones
and i've drawn the fires
that you ignite across my dried tinder
across my fallen leaves
the smoke that billows and fills the pages

i've drawn the tiger pacing the cage
the pendulum swinging across the body

i've drawn all the saints in heaven
all the angels arranged in chorus in rows
yellow suns blaring from their horns

i've drawn you in the dark
silent predator unseen but present
a constant reminder

i've drawn you in hoodie and leggings
i've drawn you in leather and lace
in time and space

i've drawn you tall like gods
like the chrysler building
like flowers falling to the ground

i've drawn you every which way i know how
upside down rightside up inside out
guts splayed widening across empty space
like the expansion of zero gravity

i've drawn you as an alien planet
one million clones in militant rows
saluting the flag of my heart

my wrist is breaking
bones grinding down from the ineffable pressure
of you

there has been nothing
that has left me feeling quite like this
a poet lost for words
forced to draw
but i refuse to shoot

Amnistía

i can see the you that lives in your head
eternally folding and mending your bed
i can see you laying and counting the sheep
restless and worried and empty of sleep

i can see you waiting for some kind of spark
lying alone on your bed in the dark
lying alone in the dark on your bed
of course i mean you that lives in your head

i too am someone who lives in my skull
with cupboards of china awaiting the bull
and when the bull comes the whole damn thing rattles
in grey panorama it battles and battles

in Guernica in restless in blood on the floor
but it's the silence come after i truly abhor
i traipse through the shards on my bare swollen feet
and the me in my head hides under my sheets

and lying alone in the dark in my bed
i think of the you that lives in your head
and maybe one day i will open my door
and throw on my rucksack and go to explore

the great range of skulls that make up a range
of mountains with faces so real and so strange
their eyes always blinking and sleeping at night
and while i meander these mountains i might

look in your eyes and see all the magic
that seeps through like beauty seeps through all the tragic
i might find a door at the cusp of your eyes
and crawl through your pupil to find you surprised

that someone has entered the room in your head
and i'll lay down beside you on your newly made bed
and i'll kiss you and love you and we'll fall asleep fast
and i'll tell you the distance i've traveled is vast

i'll tell you my stories of bulls and the war
and the light shining brightly through the cracks
                                                    in your door
and the sound of surrender and the breath of the dead
because i see the you that lives in your head

Woman, Blue Hair

there's a woman with blue hair sleeping in my closet
her clothes are on the floor the walls the ceiling
she plays me leonard cohen and lady gaga
and we sit in silence having conversations
her hair tied tight twisted she paints herself
and she lights a candle in the nucleus of my apartment
she speaks leonard cohen and lady gaga
and patiently she teaches me languages i've never dug from the cold ground

i asked her to come to denver
and she arrived on my doorstep

she tells me that she's staying here as long as she likes
she doesn't apologize and she doesn't need to

she makes me question god
and helps me find it in the thick rings of my tree
she sings like warcry and nirvana

and the mirrors are part of the conversation
the open books scattered like dead birds on the floor
the chair, the bookshelves

in this tiny room of an apartment there is a tangible physical representation in each minute detail of the war that wages in the confines of my mind and she enters in it unafraid and curious and lovely and lighting a candle in the nucleus of it all speaking cohen and gaga and sweet songs as i wake up into a new life with her unafraid as all hell

We Pretend to Be

here
nearing perfect form
do i pretend to be
something of gentleman

top hat
ascot
lovely pocket square
monocle
long tailed coat
newly shined shoes
i do look the part so well

and beneath
classic human skeleton
blue veins
red muscle
tendons fibers skin
hair nails eyeballs
i do pretend to be

and watch me walk around
the party

watch me
as i
look across the ballroom
(wood floors, glass windows
chandeliers, fire, wax, wick, etc.)
spot a female

flowing long dead hair
red dress the amalgamation
of ten thousand machine-placed
sequins

watch as i approach
muscles pulling leg
tendons working in conjunction
the cardiovascular system
in tandem with the human heart
it all moves footstep by footstep
in newly shined shoes
across the wood floors of the ballroom

and now we
meeting eyeballs
engaged
pupils expand
let in chandelier light
a legion of cheek muscles active
and we talk and smile
we pretend to be
something

and we dance
to mathematical sound
recognized by ears as pleasant
dancing
we
two human beings
in sequence through time and space
until the song
the mathematical gathered sound
ceases
and then more

and more and more and more

and we pretend it all

watch us as we pretend

and then no matter the trajectory
of following hours
eyeballs rest
beneath eyelids
automatic breathing
automatic bloodwork
and we believe we somehow changed

we believe we somehow not what we were

and maybe we believe wrong
but we believe
what we pretend to believe
and that's nice

Quickie

sometimes ya just
gotta get in
get out
bada boom
bada bing
and get on with
the rest of yer day

you know what i mean

Date With a Beautiful Woman
(Where I Turn Into a Werewolf)

when i stare across the table and i realize i am in love
and she looks at me as if she is in love with me as well
but that must be some sort of mistake there's no way
maybe it's the sushi it's gotta be the sushi
i assume everyone looks like they're in love when
they are eating sushi

i sneeze, but it sounds more like a monstrous growl
one of those sneezes that you hear someone do
and you just want to walk across the sushi bar
and slap them across their face for being obnoxious
i sneeze one of those sneezes into my arm
and i look back at her,
sugar-eyed she says "bless you."
and i think to myself that i must be blessed
but my arm so close now i see what is beginning to happen

great thick hairs begin to crawl through my skin
                                         like spiders
as my nails lengthen sharpen and blacken on my left arm
i turn my wrist, below the table, upright
                                     and black veins bulge
pulsating, i glance up in fear and she is still oblivious to me
she picks at the sushi with her chopsticks and has no clue
that i am beginning to transform

i reach for the sushi with my right arm, still normal
and say something like "this is some damn good sushi."
my hand shaking as i bring the raw fish to my salty mouth
i chew the sushi like it's the first thing i've eaten in weeks

with the desperation of a wild wolf
my teeth at war with each other
my vision begins to blur
and i see her just stare onward at me
her cheeks rosy and red her hand
reached out for my hand
the lights become harsh and great fangs
begin to grown in my mouth
the taste of blood rises from the pit
of my stomach like a monsoon
i reach my contorted hand for hers
and i hold it like a support system
my fingers tracing her wrist i start to think about her blood
i start to think about my wolf fangs
diving deep into her neck

i think about the moan it would release from her soul
like a ghost set loose out into the world, like smoke rising
like some shadow of a red balloon
rising into the atmosphere

still she looks at me like i'm the
doctor who cured her cancer
she looks at me like i'm the mailman
and it's her sixteenth birthday
my vision black and green the world is some strange jungle
and the kettle drum inside me continues
to gain and gain more
my breaths grow faint and i am still turning,
now my right arm
grown reckless and hairy thgere's no room
in my animal skull any longer
for thoughts of philosophy or poetry
or sweet women at dinner tables

and still she looks at me
like i am the man she wants to marry
and still she looks at me
like i am some realization of a dream
while inside of me demons dance
around huge bonfires
while inside of me mountains burn
and great cities are evacuated
she still looks at me, and interlacing
her soft fingers between
the dangerous clutch of my morbid claws
she speaks with pink lips
i love you
and i howl a resonating bloodlust howl
for the death inside my soul
for the eternal chase of the scattered prey
dark praise to the moon
but all she hears is
i love you too, and
this is some damn good sushi

Spies

do not trust
anyone
that you
have not seen
naked.

actually

strike that.

do not trust
anyone.

I Slept on Your Floor
in the Autumn of Your Home

i slept on your floor in the autumn of your home
in dim light we mourned the death of your year
shadows of trees against the walls like skeletal hands
you were wearing a party dress but you looked
ready for a funeral

you hosted a seance for the ghost of your happiness
you invited the whole town to come dance but our legs were
tired from trying to keep up with you
we slept in spare beds on the floor in cupboards and we dreamt
of change as you nightmared in the same space
the brick walls so redundant the smoke climbed the lines the
jester performed his manic depressive juggling act the smoke
billowed the balloons on the floor looked sad making love to the
dust your legs were white as winter

i was not here for any of this i was just the eyes of the painting
that you painted of yourself

i was the broken streamers swaying from the ceiling
like a hanged man

i was the last hope never wanted to be but there i was the angel
of death come to swing the sword

i never wanted to be
and you always wanted to be so badly

3015 Kalmia

we stood inside the abandoned house
taking in the wreckage
like pages torn from a bible
carpet pulled up
thick dust on top of empty shelves
sunlight catching broken glass windows
like a mother grabbing her wandering child's hand

you said it was so loud in there
the stories that scream in silence
the stairs that creak
and the lives that were lived and lost

and you knew to stop there
some message in a bottle
washed up on the shore
at 3015 kalmia street
and you spotted the glint of it
as we drove past
on this bleak and beautiful day

i wanted to sleep there
to stay in that house for the night
and wake up tomorrow morning
and help it regain its legacy
put a chest paddle paintbrush to its walls
and shock it back into consciousness

i don't know what i'm trying to say
except that there was something in you
that knew that there was something

to see in this abandoned house
that flashed in front of us
at forty some miles per hour

i've been taught to look at the mountains
the sky the trees the murals on the sides of buildings
but you reminded me how god hides
in the places you'd least expect to see her

I Shot a Bullet at the Mirror
and the Mirror Shot Back

i shot a bullet at the mirror and the mirror shot back
and my head hit the tile with a thunderous clack
and the clack sounded loudly such an echoing sound
and as i stared at the ceiling all the cobwebs i'd found
they reminded me time has a way to keep moving
and i found myself stuck with no patience to lose and
my patience was gone it had leaked from my brain
and it packed up its suitcase and boarded the train
and the train went to nowhere or at least so i heard
when i sat back and watched and i realized absurd
things happen and we just keep sipping our coffee
as we stare at our watch in some strange hotel lobby
that we call our existence where we never are sure
if our intentions are selfless or if they come across pure
but i'm telling you this that i learned looking up
at the ceiling of the bathroom where i swallowed my blood
that if the train that you're riding ever goes off the track
and you pick up a gun and it goes in your sack
and you go to a room with a mirror that stares
and its empty and hopeless with too many chairs
and not enough people and you look in the mirror
and you're just staring back at everything that you fear
when you pull out your gun from your oversized sack
if you shoot at the mirror it is sure to shoot back
this i know beyond reason this i know for a fact
cause i shot a bullet at the mirror and the mirror shot back

Sitting in Your Dark Living Room
While You Blowdry Your Hair

and i don't know how long these things take
but i am quickly learning
across the room
you are wearing a beautiful, flowy dress
like always
your hand is on your hip
as your other hand grips the dryer
as hot wind blows
through your manic hair
the chairs in the living room
aren't saying anything
the television
is completely off
you ask me
if i want a book to read or something
but i couldn't be happier
than sitting in your dark living room
while you blowdry your hair

Why Still So Hungry Am I

why still so hungry am i
why still so wrapped in ribbon in gauze
in ambulance
in fierce new awakening
in comedown to sugar sweet denver
and its egg crack center
why still so hungry am i
why beat the blood from the heart
banged against the brick wall
grated like cheese
why still so hungry am i
and where goes the escalators
the lack of gravity in the chamber
the people at the south pole standing upside down
and i am them
why still so hungry am i
why my boom not go boom
where my american dream
where my blonde blushing bride
my sit com wife
my day t.v. divorce court
why still so hungry am i
twenty seven
desperate afraid of white lighters
desperate afraid of basquiat cobain joplin
i escape the noose
or do i just ignore its hanging opportunity
a juicy hamburger
floating in the air
like a lightbulb swinging in a basement

why still so hungry am i
where go each branch of my plath tree
where die each planet i do not astronaut
the night sky black as the inside of my eyelids
why still so hungry am i
i go to sleep hungry now
to dream stomach acid dreams
to sleep in to wake up to move to go to die again
each night
starving
craving the dirt of the earth i can't unbury
why dear white fluffy cloud god
why still so hungry am i

Heartbreaker

and then i woke up
from what was a shitty sleep to begin with
to the sound of scratching at the door
the jiggling of a door handle
that i heard from my window

was it a burglar?
was it a bounty hunter with a gun
come to take my life in exchange for his reward?
was it a bear? come in search for scraps of food?
was it death himself reaping at my doorway
with sickle and skeletal finger taps?
an ex-lover gone mad?

i jump up and turn on my light
to see what is happening down below
my heart racing
and as i peer my hazy eyes down

i don't see anything

just the stale night of a stale porch
stale fence stale bush stale car parked in the
stale driveway

i resign to my sleepless bed
and begin to count dust particles
like a patient of dementia
recounting lost memories

isn't that just what it is sometimes?
we just so desperately want something to happen
anything to happen
for better or worse
and when nothing does
well it's enough to break your heart

Trotsky

"they have
a mountain dew
doritos
cupcake recipe,"
said Kathryn,

as Brice
bashed in
his skull
with an ice
pick.

Bees

the bees are dying
we are killing them
and i don't know how to save them

the idea of extinction
is foreign to me
i can't really
wrap my head around
how something can just
cease to exist

i mean
i understand things die
but an entire species
just gone

i just want bees
to always exist

they say
when the colonial ships
washed up on the shore
that the natives couldn't see them
simply because they didn't
understand the concept
of a ship

with bees it feels like
the opposite
i know they exist
and i understand what they are

little yellow and black creatures
flying through the air
collecting pollen
those are bees
i know that

i need to accept
that maybe you are a bee
and you could disappear from existence

i'll wander the streets of denver
a crazy bearded prophet
telling cautionary tales of when you
landed on my flower
and the pollen i gave you
and how you disappeared
despite the fact i knew you
and understood what you were
but you'll be gone
heels clacking down the hall of extinction
and no one will believe me

i just want bees
to always exist

i just need bees
to always exist

Xmas

the fan stopped spinning the
dishwasher stopped washing a long time
ago so i guess that just leaves me sitting here twiddling
my thumbs til trump jumps into temper tantrum and hits the
button
on the big
one
yeah that's me
trying to find optimism in momentary existential crisis but on
the flip side can
a flower
really grow as big as it likes if it doesn't
take a minute
to compare itself to the sky which never ends?
i'm just saying
ennui is just a fancy french word for going numb
trying to figure some stuff out but that's neither here nor there
i guess that's
what i'm getting at
the fan stopped spinning and there
is a sufficient amount of winter floating around the house
two pbr's one shaken rolled and lit partridge in the pear tree
you know
i'll get where i'm headed
i'm resilient
i'ma push through the nihilism
like the militantly happy fucker i am
so here i am you know
merry christmas
hallelujah
amen

An American Portrait

picture this:
in the center of it all is a big red house
in front of the house a man holds his wife
they smile
the woman is pregnant and happy
she looks very coy
he looks very proud to hold her
they look fairly well off
somewhere off in the background
there is a spotted dog running around
searching for something
there is a white fence around the house
the sky is blue, of course
really blue
there's some horses
very handsome horses
the grass is green and flourishing
off in the distance are hills
great hills
they go on forever
there's desert dust at their feet
there's a red convertible in the driveway
there's a beat up old truck on the road
there's something in the window
a glimmer of a light
maybe a christmas tree
maybe something secret

the clouds in the sky were made by god
a very specific god
who shines down upon this family
a very specific type of sunshine
there's a chimney on the roof
with smoke rising up out of it
it's all just as you'd imagine

you can see the brushstrokes
and the dust its collected
over the years

Blood on the American Highway

there is blood on the american highway
red paint splattered on white median lines beneath a blue sky
we run from coast to coast
we take off in the night, trunk left open, and we fly through the
eye of the needle
into the rocky mountains in search of the final sun
that sun which burns brightly dying for california
we kiss the hills along the way
we salute the cold night concrete with lit cigarettes left to ash
we don't know where we go
we just do as the green signs tell us to

the lostest of the lost pioneers
disoriented we are disoriented we follow the smoke signals
we drive right through the indian ghost the song of the past
we just blast the radio as if we could fill the sky with sound
great american rock sound
blaring guitars, raging drums, and the bass that moves
like a convertible through the wind
the sound through your head

this is our american song
rewritten and rewritten again
we search for freedom in its bars
independence in four four time
this is our american song
waking up in motel sixes with no cigarettes
and the t.v. is on for noise

and the sex through the wall
and the jingling of slot machines down the hall
and the hum of the ice machine
check out time is eleven o clock

we wrote our song into our constitution
first we decided we would be free
then we decided we needed guns
and we threw a couple to alabama
and we threw a few more to texas
and we boarded up the borders that we broke down

there are lights in fields in plains of kansas
to light the gymnasium swaying to high school dance
we move our hips like pioneers
we throw our hands up in the air
and when the music dies down
we drive to the tops of hills that look down on the nothing
and we kiss like we have to

then we're off again
down the bloody american highway
through cities and deserts and fields and mountains
and more cities and we're going where no one else has gone
at least that's what we tell ourselves

we throw on our kerouac hats
and put an eighth of ginsberg in our glove compartment
we load up our hemingways into the trunk
and we drive
we drive into the most unnatural horizon
we move down the bloody american highway
tank on e, stuck with the am radio through the worst parts of utah

we move at so many miles per hour
of course
there is blood on the american highway

Portrait of a Woman at a Gas Station

it's pitch black out
you can barely see her in the
dim haze of the lights from the
convenience store windows
and the overhead lights above her
as she pumps her gas
one hand in her black peacoat the other
grasping the handle of the gas pump.

she stares blankly at the screen
calculating her total number of gallons
of gasoline and her total cost. her eyes do not flinch.

she just stares completely blankly ahead of her.
no one else is there. it is just her.
even the clerk inside is in the back,
maybe closing a drawer or watching the news.
but it is night and it is just her
and the nothingness of three in the hollow morning

her vacant eyes stare onward
and she cannot look away from this something
this unavoidable something that comes creeping in
on us all

when the night turns worldless and empty
when the stars hide and you are left
to face the silence and yourself
alone in this giant world where
the lights beam down just
on you and there is
just you.

Simon Says

at work
in the parking lot of a
shitty kind of
morning

listening to
the opposite of
lullabies

windows rolled up
doors locked

and if i smoked
i would be smoking
now

out the front
window of my hot black
car

a man with glasses
directly across the way
from me

exits his car
and begins walking
towards the work building.

windows rolled up

"stop," i say,
he does.

"lock your doors,"
he does. he can't hear me.

"get on the roof of your
car," and he turns back around,
robotically, and steps up onto the
roof of his car.

he is skinny and awkward,
standing on the hood of a ninety-five
civic, so naturally
unnatural.

"now jump off," i say, and
he does. and shit
i'm late for work and i'm sure
he is too.

"take out your cellphone,"
and he does.
"call in sick for me,"
and he does.
"call in sick for you,"
and he does.

i tell him to climb a tree
and he can't hear me
but he can,
and he does.
he swings
like a monkey from
a branch.

"go jump in
that lake!" and
like a dog chasing after
a ball, he
obeys.

he does not look
tortured.

within someone else's will
he is peaceful and
undaunted.

he just stands there smiling
in the lake
by the parking lot
near work.

i think of all the advantages
of this situation; the
power.

i command him
never ever listen to my commands
again, and he does.

Bird #2

you pulled over
on the side of road
and you played a song
for a cow
in the middle of nowhere
i don't remember where
because it's not important
but you played that song
to that cow
in that field
in the middle of nowhere
and some may say
why the hell
would you play a jazz song
for a cow
in a field
in the middle of nowhere
but i guarantee you
that cow went back
and he or she
bragged to all the other cows
forever more
that bird pulled over
in a field
in the middle of nowhere
just to play a song
for him
or her.

Bird #1

i can just see you, charlie parker
watching television
at the stanhope hotel, hard of breath
hard of head and heart
i can see your glazed eyes
as you watched the juggler juggle
on the dorsey brothers stage show
and you juggled the drugs
with the loss of your daughter
you juggled your bebop revolution
with the aftermath
plane rides to los angeles
red eyes back to new york
days on end in a garage
you jazz players love
to lock yourself away
with the discipline of a madman
thirty-four years old
but you must have looked
twenty years older
watching the juggler juggle
on that black and white television
and you laughed
you laughed and you laughed
and you laughed until you were choking
and the baroness asked
if you needed to go to the hospital
earlier that evening
and you refused
you couldn't juggle any longer
but you knew
if you stayed where you were
you could die laughing.

This is Not a Picture Show

this is not a picture show

there are no opening credits
no haunting score of music
no rising dramatic plot

this rises and falls as it will
timelines blur
ideas are lost and sometimes

there is no scene of repentance

there is not always
a bombastic kiss
in lunar midnight
on new year's eve
this is something
more romantic
than that

this is not a picture show

this is sparks
meandering currents
inside your lockbox skull
to present you
this chaotic rock opera

you strapped to a chair
not in the audience

but on stage
you strapped to a chair
writhing

feeling your finger nails
scratching its wooden arms
and your bloody wings burst forth
splayed across the rostrum

rows of empty seats
in the house

the sun is the closest thing
to spotlight

there is no audience
only the audience of memory
a pamphlet
dirtied by footsteps
folded in half
and tucked into the back pocket
of your hard drive

there is a fade to black
but there are no end credits
this does not always end
with a wedding
or a funeral
this does not always end

this rises and falls as it will

timelines blur

ideas are lost and sometimes
they are found again

this is not a picture show
it's something much braver than that

Waiting Room

there is me
neck deep in my book
and a man beside me
chewing on his phone
and then there is death
sitting in the seat between us
when he isn't shaking
the snack machine
trying to knock loose
his bag of chips

Ambulance Song

i couldn't sleep for shit last night

i am hungry and restless and full of fire

the trees outside are dead
not seasonally dead
they are chopped down
the trees outside are brick houses
and grumpy people at a bus station
and ten million ambulances

there are so many ambulances that come down lincoln avenue
so many heart attacks and strokes and so many states of
emergency

i've learned to sleep to the sound of them
to close my eyes during never ending catastrophe
cuddling up with a baseball bat

because the ambulances just keep dancing down the line
like some weird concrete form of synchronized swimming
the most efficient and expensive taxi cab you'll ever take

it's fascinating to think that i might ride in a hearse someday and
never know

or maybe i'll be elsewhere
picking apples off the heaven tree
stealing third base with eve
in the shade

and peeping down through the marshmallow heaven clouds
i'll say hey - i'm riding in a hearse
and i'll say hey—now these fuckers care about poetry
i'll say hey i never said that! i didn't even like that guy

because everyone is best buddies with a dead poet they knew
everyone is thick as thieves with the man in the casket

i do have to say it's worth it
this life
if only for these moments
a grilled cheese sandwich
a first orgasm
sleeping in when you're a bitter shithead adult
and pissy at your inability to live the life you want

you could drown in it
you could down it like whiskey every day

life is a love song for the hedonist
death is a parade for the realist

margarine is butter for people who think death isn't real
a grilled cheese made with margarine is like a sad handjob

i'm euphoric for the opportunity to live each day
i am blessed and kind to be in this dream
the protagonist scrolling across this 4k television
i will live hard and eat the things placed before me
but you bet your ass i will burn the fat off my heart
i am holy and desperate and full of moonlight
i am hungry and restless and full of fire

i couldn't sleep for shit last night
i just tossed and turned

i closed my eyes and died in psychedelic bursts of raging color
like spirits in the river styx reaching out their decaying hands
death is the final revolution and most definitely not televised
i closed my eyes and saw a ballerina dancing on a lake of fire
she floated across the flaming pond but did not succumb to it
bulletproof to the heat she moved in rhythmic time to a song
to a song that i could not hear for it was not my song to hear
she heard something i did not know

i couldn't sleep for shit last night
i just tossed and turned

and caught up in headache i pulled out the old timey calculator
and i tallied up my problems one at a time cross-categorized
and i dug in to see what the algorithm was numbers floating
strange algebra and cosines and lines of best fit floating through
the air i realized i had a metric shit ton of problems and then i
counted my blessings

and i got too caught up in the poetry of my blessings
to care about the math of my problems

i couldn't sleep for shit last night
i just tossed and turned
i guess i'll sleep when i'm dead

Human

some of us
put our legs on
one at a time
in the morning
reattach our heads
twist them on even
if we're lucky
some of us
some of us
take time to test
our ten fingers
run them across
a piano
a keyboard
across skin
some of us
sit in front
of ourselves
and practice
our human voices
we take time
to remember
what we are
and we are all of it
we are what we need
and what we want
and it is all beautiful
but it takes time
also beautiful
but one at a time
the legs

the eyes
the elbows
the loins
we dis attach
and reattach
and it means all the same
it means all the same things
if not all the more
some of us
we work all the harder
to create our faces
and be human
some of us
some of us
some of us

Seppuku

if history has taught us anything
it's that if you're going to kill yourself off
do so in a ceremonious manner.

hang yourself from a cross
set yourself on fire
drag a dagger across your belly

and
of course
there's always poetry.

Heaven

if and when
the angels come for
me

they will have to
drag me up to the
heavens

my nails
buried deep in the
ground

desperately
holding on to this world
that i love so
dearly.

ABOUT THE AUTHOR

Brice Maiurro (he/they) is the Editor-in-Chief of South Broadway Press. Hailing from Lakewood, Colorado, they are the author of four collections of poetry, including Stupid Flowers and The Heart is an Undertaker Bee. His poetry has been published by South Florida Poetry Journal, Denverse, The Denver Post, Boulder Weekly, Suspect Press, and Poets Reading the News. Website: www.maiurro.co

ABOUT THE PRESS

South Broadway Press
is a publisher of poetry through books,
print journals, and on our online journal.

OUR MISSION

Our mission is to provide a platform for ideas that provide alternatives to the harmful systems and ideologies that we historically have and continue to live among. We are interested in work that points us towards symbiosis with not just other humans, but with all beings in this moment, all beings past, and those future beings that will be impacted by the choices we collectively, and individually, make today. We focus our attention on love as a guiding force. Not a love that only reactively supports those who have been afflicted by oppression, but a love that is willing to disrupt, disobey, and proactively prevent and redirect the potential forthcoming affliction around us. A love that is resolute in its boundaries for itself and others. A love that takes the form of dissent, resistance, and in the words of John Lewis, a love that is willing to "get into good trouble".

www.southbroadwaypress.org

OUR SEAL

Our seal is **the Bear, the Wrench, and the Quill.**

The Bear as a symbol of balancing softness with strength. The Bear as a call to approaching the caves of our internal worlds with curiosity. To slow living, and to laying witness to ourselves as not just material beings walking this Earth, but celestial beings, such as the great bear that graces the winter sky above us.

The Wrench as a symbol of disruption. A willingness to throw a wrench into the gears of fascism.

The Quill as a reminder of the adage that "the pen is mightier than the sword", and a calling to approach our work and play with that integrity and power in mind.

Our seal is also a nod to **Mutiny Information Cafe**, a bookstore, coffee shop, and community hub for over ten years now. A space that has time and again proved home for the cultivation of revolutionary ideas and the soft hearts that hold them.

www.ingramcontent.com/pod-product-compliance
Lightning Source LLC
LaVergne TN
LVHW041629070426
835507LV00008B/523